CW00642768

Comments oı

'An inspiring insight into the less well-publicised side of social care.'

'An enchanting journey into a time that no longer exists.'

'An honest tribute to Miss Martin and to life in a small East Lothian town.'

'Memories of a bygone era.'

Gift Aid

20   11111973   5705

Tenterfield

My Happy Childhood In Care

by

Margaret Irvine

© Margaret Irvine 2010

The right of Margaret Irvine to be identified as the author of this work has been asserted by her in accordance with the Copyright, Designs and Patents Act, 1988.

Published by Fledgling Press 2010
www.fledglingpress.co.uk

Printed by Exactaprint, Glasgow

ISBN-13 978-1-905916-26-9

Tenterfield

My Happy Childhood

In Care

by

Margaret Irvine

Publisher's foreword

Imagine you had 39 brothers and sisters. Children's homes and their staff are better known nowadays for the sad cases when things go wrong.

This honest and direct memoir is a wonderful reminder of how good things could be, with loving and caring staff helping children whose own families had come unstuck.

Margaret was the youngest of twelve, and her delightful story tells how good an upbringing she had under the care of Miss Martin and the excellent staff of Tenterfield House, with strong support from the local community.

Read it and I think you will soon see why I decided to publish it.

Zander Wedderburn,   Fledgling Press

Contents

Dedication

This book is dedicated to all the staff who worked in Tenterfield while I was a child in their care. I have never felt embarrassed about having been in care and have always been proud of the care that I was given; I certainly was given lots of love which I would not have received from my natural parents – there were always boundaries in Tenterfield but we children had freedom too.

I would like to thank Clare who has been behind me one hundred percent and helped with typing all my work, also her husband and girls for allowing their mum to help me with this task.

Thank you Clare.

Many thanks also to Neil Murray of the Aston Martin Heritage Trust.

Acknowledgements

Many people have helped in the making of this book but special thanks go to Sheila Millar and her archivists at East Lothian Library Services, Simon Kesley of Kesley's Bookshop, Dr Joy Hendry of Chapman Publishing, Mrs Mary Russell for the picture of her parents, Lord and Lady Haddington, Professor Ian Campbell and my brother Angus. My husband Gordon too for encouraging me not to give up! Finally, and most importantly, I wish to thank everyone who contributed memories (which helped my own), and photographs, all of which helped make the book what it is.

Margaret Irvine June 2010

1 Beginnings

I was born in Edinburgh on the nineteenth of November nineteen forty six, the youngest of twelve children, to John and Josephine Irvine nee Horne. After leaving Simpson's Maternity Hospital – based at the old Royal Infirmary in Edinburgh I was taken to the family home in Park View, Prestonpans, East Lothian. I can only look back now and imagine how difficult life must have been for my mother especially having no help from my father. I never knew him. I remember one of my older sisters – Nancy – telling me all about my father and from what she told me he seemed to spend most of his time drinking in the local pubs.

As I was born just after the war, food was scarce and there were no Social Security benefits available as there are today, so you can understand why life became difficult for some very large families like ours. When I was around two years old our family was brought to the attention of the local authorities as we (the younger children) were often found wandering the streets while our mother searched the local pubs for our father, trying to find him before he spent all his money on drink. She needed money for food and heat but it was a regular occurrence for her to have to go looking for him.

As the authorities were on the way to collect us seven younger children my sister Nancy took me into our garden and rolled me up in an old carpet in an attempt to hide me. She waited until I fell asleep and then went inside to wait for the Welfare Officers as they were called then. When they noticed one child was missing they asked Nancy where I was but she refused to tell them; however thankfully I was found. She always told me that she had wanted to keep me. We were all placed in the Children's Shelter in Edinburgh until a suitable children's home could be found to accommodate us. At the same time we were made Wards of Court, which meant that we would not see our parents again until we were very much older and able to decide for ourselves whether we wanted to see them. Our parents received a letter from the authorities regarding the decision.

Tenterfield House - a children's home - was found in Haddington, East Lothian, not far from Prestonpans. I don't remember anything at all about the Matron who ran the home when we first arrived but when I was about four a new Matron – Miss Martin – took charge of Tenterfield. My older brother Angus tells me that the previous Matron was never as nice as Miss Martin and that she left quite abruptly. He also remembers that she was quite young, perhaps around twenty five and engaged so perhaps this was the reason she left. We were one of the first families in Tenterfield after it was taken over by the now defunct Midlothian, East Lothian & Peebles County Council .

The new Matron was here and I did not think much of her looks or appearance. She wore a grey pleated skirt and jacket, pink shirt and tie and black lace up shoes and also had very short hair. I thought to myself "What do we have here?" but my fears were soon allayed. Miss Dorothy Kathleen Martin was born in nineteen hundred and six in Chelsea, North London. Her father was Lionel Walker Birch Martin, the co-founder of the Aston Martin car group. Miss Martin did not talk much about her father only saying that he liked to race cars and won many trophies. As we children became more comfortable with Miss Martin we would ask her questions about her childhood.

One particular question we liked to ask was why did she want to look after this ever-growing family of children. Her reply was that as a child she had had a Nanny and on one of her daily walks with her Nanny she had met a large group of children from the local children's home being taken for a walk also. She had asked her Nanny why the other Nannies had so many children with them and when it was explained to her that these children did not live with their parents she decided there and then that she would look after all the children in the world. We were the lucky ones who did receive the privilege of being cared for by this wonderful woman.

Miss Martin had been given the authority to pick her own staff and along came Miss Florence McDean whom we renamed 'Mackie' or 'Nanna Dean' to the younger children. There was also Mary who was a gem too. Both Mackie and Mary had worked with Miss Martin in North Berwick. We also had other staff to help with our care – domestics, laundry staff, a cook and a sewing lady had all worked in the home prior to Miss Martin's arrival and they stayed on and worked with her. The gardener Mr McLaren lived in a tied cottage in the grounds. They were all to play a big part in my upbringing. As I became older questions such as "Do I have parents?" and "If so why was I in Tenterfield?" occurred to me. Miss Martin would sit me down, often on her knee, and explain my past to me in a way that I as a child could understand. She told me about the circumstances my parents had been in and how it was not suitable for children to be brought up in that way. She would also say that we were the lucky ones to have been taken out of such hardship and to have a chance of a much better life. Miss Martin also made it clear to me that this was not our fault and if necessary she would remind me of my parents' situation. She was always there when you needed her.

We all became known as Miss Martin's children – never children from Tenterfield Home and we all loved this fact. We were brought up to always respect our house and ourselves and of course, each other.

2 Tenterfield Life

Once I remember some of us older children going for a cycle run under Mackie's supervision. We cycled so far that we all got lost and Mackie phoned home to let Miss Martin know. She was not too impressed with the situation and informed the police who found us and escorted us home safely. Mackie was told that under no condition must she do that again! And of course she didn't.

Mackie was also a very artistic person; she drew many pictures for the younger children and they would paint in the colours. The older children would also try and draw just like her; I'm afraid I wasn't one of them but many a child did learn to draw well. Miss Martin always said all children are good at something as long as they are given the opportunity and she made sure that we were given opportunities. In the evenings when the weather was bad the playroom was a hive of activity. The older children did basket weaving and I enjoyed this very much. The weaving material would have been soaking in the bath for hours, and we would take it from the bath, give it a good shake and run with it dripping, all the way downstairs to the playroom, shaking it over each other. We would arrive at the playroom and begin weaving but only if we wanted to. If we didn't we could read or do something else to amuse ourselves in the playroom.

The best place to be with Mackie was outdoors; this lady was a free spirit – our 'Maria'[1] – she loved the freedom of being outside and would always organise rounders, football or any other sport you could think of, never being short of two teams as there were so many children in Tenterfield. We would also spend time walking in the surrounding hills, being taught about the birds we saw and the rabbits and hares, racing up and down the hills and also learning all about the wild flowers. Mackie was a walking encyclopaedia and there was very little she did not know.

When the snow was on the hills we would all be eager to get home from

---

[1] From The Sound of Music 1965

church on a Sunday, have lunch then get changed out of our Sunday clothes, grab our sledges which were homemade, and head for the hills. What fun we had – we spent many a happy hour up there taking turns to sit on the sledge or even riding two at a time; flying downhill it was like total freedom. When Mackie and the other members of staff had a turn on the sledges all the children would laugh as they raced each other down the hill with us shouting their names. We would return home hungry and very happy, all trying to tell Miss Martin at the same time about the afternoon's events.

Mackie also had the job of looking after the girls aged from six to fourteen. She would get 'her' girls up at seven o' clock and the older ones would help her get the younger ones ready before going off to the bathroom to wash and do our teeth. We would make our beds and then it would be downstairs for breakfast. This time of day seemed to be very quiet; maybe some of the children were still half asleep from the busy evening the night before.

Breakfast consisted of porridge, cereal, eggs sometimes boiled, poached or scrambled, toast and marmalade and a cup of tea. While we were having our breakfast the staff would have theirs, as Miss Martin always supervised mealtimes. Mealtimes always began by saying Grace and as the children got older they would start by saying "For what we are about to receive" to which the rest of the children would reply "May the Lord make us truly thankful, AMEN!" However when we played outside we had our own version which was "One word is as good as ten, tuck in, AMEN!" If only Miss Martin knew!

Mackie would walk the younger girls to school with Mary who was in charge of the boys. They treated us like their own broods and when you reached the age of eight, if Mackie or Mary thought you were ready then you could go to school on your own and Mackie or Mary would let Miss Martin know their decision. The older children often walked with Mackie and Mary and sometimes one or another would call in for their friends en route. We were encouraged to make friends outwith Tenterfield and our friends would often come to Tenterfield for tea and we would go to their homes.

When the staff returned home from the school run there was always plenty for them to do. They would check our play clothes and get them ready for us returning from school. They often helped with each other's tasks, wash the tables and set them for lunch and then have a well-earned break in their sitting room before it was time to set off again to collect all us children from school for lunch. They then took us back to school and repeated the same tasks all over again until it was time to collect us at home time. When all the children returned home for the day it would be up to our rooms to change into our play clothes, hanging up our school clothes in the wardrobe and getting our homework ready.

After tea the younger children would go to the staff sitting room to do their homework and the older children would do theirs with Miss Martin. When homework was over we would have an hour of television then out into the field to play until your bedtime was called. At weekends, bedtime and in the evening a bell was used to call the children in, as we would be here, there and everywhere – it was a very large playing field we had. As you got older supper time was added to your three meals a day. This was usually cocoa, toast and jam and the member of staff responsible that day would decide what we were having; it was usually something good! I remember that one time it was Mackie's turn to make supper and she reckoned that Tenterfield had the very first chip shop as she made chips with vinegar and handed them out the pantry window to us. We all sat outside and ate them – I think Miss Martin must have been on holiday as chips were never usually on the menu. At the weekends we stayed in bed a little longer but not much as many of the children were in the school football, rugby or hockey teams (I was in the hockey team) so we had to get to school again for our matches.

On Sunday mornings we attended the West Church of Scotland in Haddington. After breakfast we would all be dressed in our Sunday best, all in line waiting for our penny for the collection. Miss Martin took us all to church; we filled the first two pews in the church and it never failed that someone would drop their penny. Often the Minister would pick it up and hand it back to the child, usually with a kind comment although Miss Martin would have a quiet word later with the child reminding them to be careful with their penny!

After the collection was taken the younger children went to Sunday School and the rest of us went home with Miss Martin. A member of staff would collect the younger ones later and bring them home in time to change for lunch. Until recently I was unaware that part of Miss Martin's job was to bring the children up in the particular faith that their parents requested. I personally found this strange having been more or less abandoned by my parents but Miss Martin made sure that those children whose parents did request a particular faith had their wishes honoured. I remember one boy who was Catholic and was taken to the chapel each week until he was old enough to attend himself. I believe that this was an indication of the type of person Miss Martin was – open, fair and willing to accommodate every race and religion in our home at Tenterfield. As an adult now I am beginning to understand certain things about Miss Martin. She respected each family's own faith, ignoring her own faith which was Church of England. The fact that she was never able to worship in her own church never seemed to bother her.

After church and lunch we would all be dressed in our play clothes for a walk in the hills. Sometimes Miss Martin would come with us with her dog Patch – a white and brown cocker spaniel. I think Patch was our first dog.

He came to Tenterfield at around fourteen weeks old and was absolutely gorgeous; a little bundle of fun with big eyes staring at you. He must have thought he was in heaven with all these children to fuss over him.

Patch having a rest

Patch soon settled into our very large family and often the older children would take him for a walk. He was never allowed into the children's playing field until he had been taken for a walk which I now understand was to ensure he did not foul in our play area. After his walk he would always run to the playing field as he knew where we children would be and we often chased him around the field. He could be a bit of a pest if we were playing rounders but then someone would just take him in to Miss Martin where he would lie beside the coal fire if it was on. If not then he would lie in his bed – he was the best exercised dog in Haddington.

After many years of Patch being part of our family he seemed to become very quiet. Miss Martin gave him some time to rest in the hope that peace and quiet would help him. He stayed in her sitting room, only going out when Miss Martin took him in her car to exercise away from the bustle of Tenterfield. Things were not looking too good for him and the children were always asking Miss Martin how he was. He was taken to the vet and poor Patch never returned. After tea that evening Miss Martin brought all of us children and staff together to tell us that Patch had died. One child began to cry then another and another until we were all crying, staff included. This was my very first experience of death and it took some time to get over Patch's death. We all helped each other and Miss Martin.

Time went by and Miss Martin announced that she would be bringing home another cocker spaniel and he would be here when we arrived home from school. She was true to her word and again we met another small bundle of fun. This dog was called Paddy and he was white with black patches with the same fun loving nature as Patch. He too settled into his new family and we soon had him up in the hills with us and in our playing field chasing our ball. All Miss Martin's children were so excited yet again. These two dogs seemed very special dogs with much understanding of children: after all, there were so many of us for them to put up with.

One time whilst playing in our field I fell and skint my knee. Someone ran for Mackie who came at once and carried me to the upstairs bathroom where the Dettol was kept. The Dettol was diluted with hot water and she gave my knee a good clean. With the whole entourage looking on I had to put on a very brave face (which I did) and a plaster was applied, my knee was kissed better and we were all sent back out to play.

Our health was always important and the staff noticed if any of us were unwell. Our G.P. Dr. Russach was very nice, it amazed me how he knew all the children by name. He used to come to Tenterfield and have afternoon tea with Miss Martin and discuss the health of the children. I used to see him on some of these visits as my feet were on the broad side and he recommended that I go to the Princess Margaret Hospital in Edinburgh to see the orthopaedic doctor there.

An appointment was made and I was given a day off school and driven to the hospital by Miss Martin. I remember thinking "What's all the fuss about? I can walk, run and kick a ball!" I had my feet measured and was sent home to return when special foot splints had been made for me. When they arrived and I was shown how to put them on we all had a laugh as I looked like a waddling penguin when I tried to walk in them.

Thank goodness I only had to wear them in bed but after a few weeks I just could not bear wearing them any longer. The sides were made of metal with leather straps to hold them on to your feet. When I turned over in bed they were very uncomfortable so I used to take them off. When Miss Martin discovered what I was doing she used to come and check every night before she went to bed that I still had them on. I remember pleading with her to ask our doctor to take these things away and she said she would speak with him. To my delight he agreed saying they were not going to help my feet if I didn't keep them on, and to this day my feet are still as broad, one more than the other.

Like all children we had our share of childhood illnesses but sometimes a child would become seriously ill and I remember one such occasion when one boy was very ill with pneumonia and our G.P. decided to have him nursed at home. He organised a nurse to come from the local hospital – Roodlands – to nurse him by day, and another nursed him overnight. All the equipment which might have been needed came too and I remember him being moved from the sickroom to a little bedroom just off Miss Martin's sitting room so that she too could keep an eye on him. We would be sitting in our sitting room with the television down low, all aware that we must be just like little mice until he regained his strength. With this level of care it was not long before he was back with us to Miss Martin's delight, and to ours too.

In the winter our G.P. would recommend to Miss Martin that we should all be given malt, castor oil and senna pods. Almost every child lined up voluntarily to take the malt but the staff had to come looking for us to administer the castor oil and senna pods – no wonder - they tasted disgusting. Miss Martin caught on to her disappearing children and the malt began to be handed out after the senna and castor oil which solved that problem. When I consider how many children lived in Tenterfield (around forty at any one time) it is surprising there were not many more illnesses; we seemed to have been given excellent health care.

On one occasion there was a stay in hospital for six of us (myself included). We were taken to The Sick Kids in Edinburgh to have our tonsils taken out and were all put into a room together. We had such fun before our operations that you would have thought we were at home but that soon changed. While one of us was in theatre being operated on the next was being prepped. When we all came round, a little sore and very quiet, it was good to see Miss Martin's face.   She helped the hospital staff, feeding us with jelly and icecream.

We were only in for a few days then we all went home – I think the nursing staff were glad to see us go but in a nice way.   On arriving home the other children were ready with so many questions – "What was it like in hospital?", "Did we play?", "What did we get to eat?", "Were our throats sore?" – so many people to tell.   Within a few days though, everything was back to normal.

3 Quarantine

I remember an occasion when one child in Tenterfield contracted an infectious disease and was immediately put in the sickroom. The doctor arrived that same morning to check her over and when the diagnosis was given and the disease was found to be contagious we were all quarantined for four to six weeks (staff and children). We were not allowed to pass the boundary walls of Tenterfield. This procedure was used at least twice that I can remember during my lifetime in Tenterfield. Miss Martin looked after any children in the sickroom herself and she distanced herself from all the other children at this time as far as she possibly could, in order to minimise the spread of infection.

Another illness to come to Tenterfield was dysentery which could have run rife throughout the house if Miss Martin had not had the medical knowledge she had. I remember Dr. Russach telling her that if it hadn't been for her quick thinking, separating the ill child from the rest of us immediately, then things might have been a lot worse.

Of course the remainder of the children had to be told that there would be no school, church or sports matches at the weekend until our quarantine of six weeks was over. The other children cheered but I was devastated as I played for the school team on Saturday mornings and for Haddington Ladies in the afternoon. I was only fourteen at the time and just lived for my hockey. There was no pleading with anyone this time; we were allowed to play outside in our field – thank goodness for that – and I would also practice my hockey moves outside in the playing field.

Miss Martin decided that those of us at school had to continue with lessons throughout our quarantine which didn't go down too well with some of the children. In the afternoon, before tea, we would be given lessons in reading, writing and arithmetic with Mackie, Mary, Helen or other staff members hearing the younger ones' reading. This routine took place Monday to Friday while we were in quarantine but we did get a slightly longer playtime than we would have got at school! At one time I thought that Miss Martin must have been a teacher as she seemed to have a huge amount of knowledge but I later discovered that she had been educated at a boarding school in England. I never felt that my education suffered when we had these long spells away from school and I suspect that it was Miss Martin's private tutoring which helped most of her children stay apace with their friends at school.

Every year we would have at least two frauleins from Switzerland come to stay with us to learn English. The first two were friends of Mackie whom she had met while working as a nanny there. One thing led to another and Mackie had asked if they could come to Tenterfield to work for one year. Permission had to come from the Council who were legally responsible for Tenterfield and after

One of our many frauleins

meetings with Miss Martin it was decided they could come. I remember the first two – Fraulein Myre and Fraulein Krumyre. What perfect English they seemed to speak. One had brought their guitar with them and off we all were again, learning Swiss songs with some of the children picking up their language quite well too. Miss Martin often came down to the playroom to listen to our Swiss songs especially nearer to Christmas when we all sang 'O Tannenbaum'.

Miss Martin always had pride written all over her face and we children thought we were extra clever singing in a different language. 'The Frauleins' as we named them settled into our home life very well. They too enjoyed the outdoor life. When their year was almost up there was some sadness but they took many pictures and lots of happy memories home with them. We were also told that there would be another two frauleins coming, as indeed they did.

The frauleins were always quite amazed at how we children (being so many of us) were allowed to express ourselves freely and safely. For example we were allowed to climb trees, make houses from the newly cut grass, play on the swings, roundabout, sand-pit or just laze around in the sunshine if we wanted. Yes, there were rules as most families have and we were no exception. We

were taught to learn from our mistakes –
there were certain trees we were not
allowed to climb and it was always
explained why.

Mary, who was in charge of the
boys, also received great respect from
them. She would take them down to the
River Tyne where they would all play in
the water – lots of towels needed on
those days. This was well before
Haddington got its own swimming pool.
Some of the staff who looked after the
very young ones would put two children,
sometimes three, into one pram and walk
with them down to feed the ducks at the
river. The younger ones were never left
out; they too left Tenterfield and often
got to see the outside world just like the

older ones. Later in life (I think she was about eighty years of age), Mary told me that she remembers having her hair permed for the first time and when one of her boys saw it he roared with laughter. When she asked him why he was laughing he said "Your hair looks like a bird's nest!" Mary's reply to that was "As long as they don't think it is a nest and try to lay their eggs in it, I'll be all right." She didn't take offence to this remark but was amused by it.

When Miss Martin thought we were old enough to earn our pocket money rather than just being given it we would do small jobs in the house. These jobs were not difficult: we did things like help take the dirty clothes to the laundry, put the younger children's shoes in their cubby holes, tidy the cleaning cupboard and one person had to clean her father's trophies. The jobs would be alternated every month. I just hated cleaning her father's trophies – some were almost as big as me. My favourite job was tidying the cleaning cupboard. We soon learned that in performing these tasks we were not just earning our pocket money but learning that we had to do tasks we didn't like as life was going to be like that in the future. Of course, as usual, Miss Martin was right.

Every Saturday after lunch was when we were given our pocket money. We would all be sitting discussing what we were going to spend our money on, listening for the jingle of the pocket money box which Miss Martin would bring down the stairs, having already counted all the money needed. We could hear her coming nearer. On Saturdays we could go to the cinema and also have enough money left for some sweets or to buy our favourite comics or perhaps a birthday card for a friend. We were always encouraged to use our own money for items like this. I remember one Saturday sitting chatting about what I was going to do with my money and when my turn came Miss Martin asked me how much of my pocket money I wanted this week. My answer was "One shilling and sixpence, my usual amount." I said. "No" came the reply, "I will give you half as you have not saved much these last few weeks." This was a hard but valuable lesson for me as I had to choose what to spend my smaller than usual amount of money on. Miss Martin also said "No matter how much you save, that little amount will turn into a larger amount when you keep saving." – a lesson I have never forgotten. To this day I am grateful for that advice, I hope I have passed this onto my own children and think I have.

As I write this it is Easter 2009 and this brings to my mind what the preparations for Easter were like for us children at Tenterfield. It was a special day for us and we were all given a hard-boiled egg to paint. I remember cutting an old piece of wool up to make hair and then painting a lovely smiling face. After church on Easter Sunday we would have lunch and each of us would be given a chocolate Easter egg. These would all be broken up and put into a very large tin then shared out every day until all the chocolate was finished. We were also presented with a very large egg about two feet high and almost as wide. Miss Martin asked the gardener to buy a new hammer to break it with; it was placed on a new sheet on the playroom floor and smash! it was all in little pieces... This too was put away and shared out until it was all gone.

We would all go up into the hills – the children, Miss Martin, Mackie, Mary and the frauleins, and I am sure Patch or Paddy would have been with us too. We would all roll our hard boiled eggs down the hill; it was a great time for us children and after the excitement of Easter the summer holidays were not too far away.

Tyninghame House

To us at Tenterfield summer holidays meant four weeks away from home in a little village by the sea called Tyninghame, only nine miles from Haddington where we camped on Lord and Lady Haddington's estate. When the school holidays arrived the excitement would begin. We would have one week at home, four weeks at camp and then only a week until school began again. Prior to us setting off on holiday Miss Martin would have been to see the Haddingtons to discuss the erecting of the tents which was done for us by local guides and scouts. We would be at home preparing our clothes and also helping with the younger children who got very excited.

About two days before we were due to leave for Tyninghame a huge van would appear to collect the springs from our beds (Miss Martin had the local joiner build bunk beds for camp in which the spring bases of our beds fitted.) This meant that for the last couple of nights at home before we went on holiday we had to sleep on our mattresses on the floor. The fun we had and the pillow fights were fantastic and all because we were spending four weeks at camp. When our final day at home arrived we would all help to take our mattresses to the waiting van. Some of the smaller children sat on them while the older children pulled the mattresses downstairs all screeching with laughter. Soon the van was full to the brim, the food had gone ahead, everything was ready and we the children were waiting for the bus to come and pick us up. It seemed to take forever although the garage was just around the corner from Tenterfield. When the bus arrived we were all as high as kites (the staff were secretly too – as they came with us). We would all pile onto the bus as Miss Martin counted us saying "We don't want to leave anyone behind!" Miss Martin did not travel on the bus with us; she drove her own car to camp, as this would be used in emergencies if there were any, and also to take the laundry home on a Friday and bring back clean clothes and linen.

Mackie, Mary and Miss
Martin with the laundry

A Tyninghame horse and some more laundry!

We would sing all the way to Tyninghame and on arrival could not get off the bus quickly enough to inspect what would be our new home for the next four weeks. There would be six of us sharing each tent – three sets of bunks in each tent and we often swapped from the lower to higher bunks on a Friday when the beds were changed.

Our first night under canvas was always a night to remember – probably more so for the staff – but we soon settled in. We would be very tired the next morning but up we got, washed in cold water, did our teeth and into the marquee for breakfast. The tables were all set for us. Instead of our usual square tables at home there were long trestle tables with ever so long benches which seemed strange at first but we soon became used to this way of eating. After breakfast we would take our plates outside for them to be washed. We were not allowed to help wash up as the sinks were set up beside the huge fire which was kept burning all day.

Today I would liken the fire to a very large barbeque with lots of grills on top to hold the very large pots which were used to cook with. Potatoes, vegetables and everything else we ate was cooked on this fire. After breakfast it was time to sit down and discuss what the day's events would be. Would it be swimming at the beach, beachcombing, a long walk along the beach? We would put ourselves into groups according to what we wanted to do that day – swimming at the beach was always very popular.

On Saturdays we still got our pocket money and this we would spend in the seaside town of North Berwick which used to have a Woolies[2], ideal for your pick'n'mix sweets. We also spent some time on the beach there too and at the outdoor swimming pool. We would arrive back at camp in time for tea. Baked beans on toast, fresh fruit and lots of juices to drink. Food was still important to us: there were certain things which just could not be cooked on a fire but we were still well fed.

These summer days seemed long with lots of sunshine well into the evening. After teatime we would be outside our tents, sitting in the sunshine or playing rounders, tennis or football until it was time for bed. I remember

---

[2] Woolworths

that with all the fresh air we had we would all be very tired and would go to sleep without any singing, just our usual cry of "Goodnight" to all the staff.

Uncle Willie (Merriliees) with us at Tyninghame

On one occasion, camping during our Tyninghame holidays, I remember the weather being so bad that we children were unable to play outside.

Lord and Lady Haddington

We were stuck inside our marquee, bored and quite miserable. Somehow Lady Haddington arranged for us to have a television rigged up to the electricity supply and placed in the marquee. I have no idea how this was achieved as we camped quite a distance away from the house but I remember watching *The White Heather Club* and *The Kilt is my Delight*. Our dancing teacher, and the boys' gym teacher, Stanley Wilkie danced in *The Kilt is my Delight* which is why we watched it.

Before we were allowed to go near any water we had to learn to swim. This took place back home at Tenterfield. We would lie over a stool and do all the actions – what a sight and a laugh that was! But this was Miss Martin's way and when she felt we seemed capable of going near water then we were taken to the outdoor pool in North Berwick and let me tell you this pool was *not* warm!

We were taken, one by one, into the water. Miss Martin would put a belt round your waist; attached to this was a long rope which Miss Martin held on to. We fell for this next part all the time – she would look up to the sky, your eyes would follow hers then suddenly, a little tug on the rope and off you went.

In the sea

All your lessons learned on dry land were put into practice but at least you learned how to swim. Miss Martin made sure that for our seaside holidays we would be safe near water.

Again, when we reached a certain age we were asked if we would like to go out on the North Berwick fishing boats. I remember jumping at the chance and said I would love to go. I almost changed my mind on discovering I would have to be up at two o' clock in the morning. Miss Martin was also up as she drove us there. It was very exciting being out with the fishing fleet but I was glad to get home. I didn't jump at that chance again as boats were not much to my liking but other children went often. It never occurred to me how all these events happened they just did.

Me (on the left) aged about nine

The holidays were a great time for all the children and we talked about them for weeks after.

4 School days

I went to the Knox primary school in Haddington when I was five. I was five in November and started school just after the Christmas holidays. I enjoyed my primary school very much. At first we sat at our desks, a bit like little mice for the first week or two, afraid of the unknown, but we soon settled in. No matter what we were doing in the classroom, if the headmaster came in we would greet him by saying "Good morning/afternoon Mr. Anderson!" He was the headmaster for Knox Academy too.

In the summer months if the weather was nice we would take our chairs out to the playground and do our schoolwork there. On other days we would push our desks to the side of the classroom and perform our 'music and movement' exercises accompanied by instructions from the radio. This was an educational program designed for primary school children which we found to be quite good fun but we were always told to take it seriously.

At Tenterfield once breakfast was over Mackie would get her girls ready for school, we all went down to the back door when we were dressed to collect our 'play-piece' which was always some form of fruit – no crisps or sweets. We all received free milk at school too, as did all primary age children. Tenterfield children always wore school uniform of navy skirt, white blouse, blue blazer, blue and white tie, white socks and well polished black shoes. For rainy days we wore gabardine raincoats with hoods for the girls. I was always proud to wear my uniform and we also had to have kits for gym, hockey, rugby, football and netball.

If we misbehaved at school Miss Martin would be called and was often at the school on the behalf of one child or another. She would make it clear to the headmaster that they had to work together to help the children. Many of the Tenterfield children had never seen the inside of a school in their lives and had not been taught any boundaries but after children settled at Tenterfield it seemed to follow that they settled at school too. We all went home to Tenterfield for lunch and I remember asking Miss Martin if I could have my lunch at school as it always seemed such a long walk there and back. She explained that if she allowed me to have lunch at school then others from Tenterfield would also want to do this which would mean there would not be enough lunches at the school for the children who came from the outlying villages surrounding Haddington who were unable to go home for lunch. She always explained to us her reasons for saying no and her explanations were almost always accepted.

When we reached the age of seven or eight, depending on each child, we would walk to school ourselves or be allowed to call in for our school friends but often we would still choose to walk with Mackie or Mary. When we reached the age of twelve we were sent to the Knox Institute for one year for our 'Qualifying Studies' which were needed for entrance into Knox Academy. Here they studied Latin, physics and all that clever academic stuff. 'A' was the highest grade you could achieve and I think I received a 'C' grade which meant I qualified for Commercial Studies – I didn't like that at all and remember being put into a 'D' class - this stood for Domestic Sciences which I enjoyed very much. The Qualifying School was a very good way for children to discover what they were good at.

When our classes were decided it was off to the Academy. I was in my element there playing hockey and netball and taking part in athletics although I still had to study all the academic subjects too. I settled into high school very well, having some of the children from my primary school in classes helped tremendously.

All Miss Martin's children knew how to behave themselves at school, and if we misbehaved then the headmaster would phone her and I know for a fact that a lecture from Miss Martin was far worse than being belted at school. The belt was over and done with very quickly but oh, her lecture on how to behave at school and how important an education was…. We would agree with her and promise to do our best not to misbehave again…. She was right, as always.

We did a lot of sports at school and I seemed to excel at them. From primary school age I would always win any race I was in, I remember the prize was always a very large bar of chocolate. Miss Martin always attended our sports day along with other members of Tenterfield staff. In high school the prizes were medals and I came home with many of them. On one occasion Miss Martin was watching one of my high school races and beside her was a teacher who remarked to her "My, that girl runs like the wind!" Her smile was huge as she replied "Margaret is one of my children."

When I was fourteen I played hockey for the school on a Saturday morning and I loved playing in the team. When any of the Tenterfield children were chosen for the school teams and showed that they were committed to their sport then Miss Martin would buy all the equipment they needed. I was driven into Edinburgh by Miss Martin to Lilywhites sports shop to be kitted out with all I needed for the hockey team. I remember kneeling on the shop floor as my skirt had to be a certain length and this was how it was measured. I was left-handed but back then there were no left-handed hockey sticks so I had to learn to play with my right hand which I coped with very well. Miss Martin also paid for my boots, socks and tee shirt too.

One Saturday we were sitting having lunch when I noticed the older sister of one of my friends passing the dining room window. Lunchtime was not the time to call at Tenterfield but Joy had a very important question to ask Miss Martin. Joy was the captain of Haddington Ladies Hockey team and their left-winger was ill and could not play that day. She asked if it was possible for me to play that day. I sat silently crossing my fingers and quietly pleading for the answer to be yes. It did not take long for Miss Martin to come to me with the question and before she had completed it I said "Yes!" saying it would keep me out of mischief which Miss Martin agreed with. So for a long time I played school hockey on a Saturday morning and for the ladies team on a Saturday afternoon.

Miss Martin knew the potential of all her children and sport was certainly mine. She asked a local joiner to build four hurdles and a high jump so that I and any other child who wanted to could practise in our playing field. I would hurdle and jump until my legs told me to stop and then dismantle the jump and hurdles with help from another child and put them in our Pavilion for another day.

High school was a bit frightening at first but I soon got used to it. At least there were different subjects to keep you interested and we moved from class to class which was a novelty at first. Classes included lots of sports and Scottish country dancing and the sport and dancing became some of my favourite subjects. I remember sitting in geography one day looking out of the window at a hockey match being played outside. A piece of chalk came flying through the air and hit me on the head – it wasn't sore but certainly made me pay attention to the teacher for a while (this often happened to me!).

My schooldays were very enjoyable although I never became Dux.

I did win many medals for running which gave points to the house I belonged to. My house was called 'Trapraine' and throughout the year points were given for academic work as well as for achievement at sports.

Mr. Wilkie taught both the boys and girls Scottish country dancing. He was a perfectionist and I think this was maybe because he used to dance in *The Kilt is My Delight*. He was so light on his feet and had a very slender figure for a man. He was a good teacher and I think the boys got on well with him, he even taught rugby and I don't know how he managed this being quite small and slim but he is remembered fondly.

Miss P. Adamson was the girls' gym teacher; she taught hockey and netball and would arrange tournaments against other schools in East Lothian - North Berwick High, Preston Lodge, Dunbar High and one time, a private school from Edinburgh although I don't know how that came about. I was in the hockey team and I remember the private school team being quite timid and that they thought we were a rough bunch. We weren't, as we knew Miss Adamson would not think twice about dropping a player who did not play to the rules, and as I loved my hockey I always stuck to the rules.

Miss Johnston was our sewing teacher and she always had a problem trying to teach me to sew as I was left-handed. She had to turn my work upside-down so that we were both sewing in the same direction whenever she helped me. Sewing was something else that I seemed to be good at during my schooldays and I always got good marks for my sewing. During the time I attended Knox Academy the teachers wore black gowns and I sometimes felt that when pupils saw this form of uniform, the teachers and Headmaster were automatically given the respect they were due.

I remember one day in high school being asked by the headmaster to 'run' over to the primary school with a note for one of the teachers. Of course I took him literally and began running the moment he handed the note to me. It was quite a distance from our high school to the primary and when I returned, breathless and happy, there he was waiting for me, strap in hand, to punish me for running in school. Being left-handed I would often put my left hand out when being punished by the strap for some misdemeanour or other but he would always ask for my right hand saying 'I know you are left-handed!' Although I was to be punished he still wanted me to be able to continue to write. I never felt resentful when he belted me and always thought he was a strict but fair man.

Our school playing field was adjacent to the Sheriff of Haddington's home and when our ball was invariably kicked over the wall into his garden he was not amused! Mind you he kept the most beautiful old car I have ever seen in his driveway so no wonder he became annoyed. I was often the one who was asked to run in and retrieve the ball (even if I had not been playing) as I was the fastest runner in Tenterfield. I would sneak in, heart in my mouth, hoping the ball had not gone far. If I could see it near the house then I would leave it but usually I managed to find it and get out of his garden before he realised anything had happened.

5 Bath Nights

Our bath nights were every night, hair washed every Friday and checked for nits, lotion applied if necessary and kept on overnight. I had long hair through choice and the bone comb was a nightmare going through my hair. I never once told anyone about my thinking that "If my hair was short it would not be so painful". Girls were allowed to have their hair long if they wished. The younger children were bathed first and their staff washed the baths out for the next set of children. This routine was always used until all the children were bathed. Older 'children' were allowed to bath in the staff bathroom or even Miss Martin's when she was not using it – I think this happened when she went on holiday.

I remember on one occasion the boiler seemed to stop and would not start again.   The boiler supplied all our heating and hot water so on that particular night bath night was in the laundry room!   We called it this but it was really a separate building with two rooms in it.   One was for the washing with pulleys hanging from the ceiling which were used when the weather was bad.   This room also housed the irons and a special machine for pressing the sheets.

The other room was full of Belfast sinks.   I think there were at least six along one of the walls plus one washing machine and a very big spin dryer. Miss Martin was glad that the laundry had its own hot water system as she said that the children could all be bathed in the big sinks. What a sight it was – all of us getting ready in the house, collecting our soap bags with our own toiletries, towel and facecloth. We brushed our teeth in the house and then ran across the courtyard in our slippers to the laundry, carrying our pyjamas and dressing gowns, girls first of course.

Mackie had filled all the sinks up with hot water and she told us that we could splash as much as we liked as the floor was stone with a drain in the middle of the floor for all the water to run into. What fun we all had that bath night! After getting dried and dressed in our pyjamas, dressing gowns and slippers it was another quick sprint across the courtyard and into the staff sitting room to have our hair dried and supper.

6 Fire Drill

Our fire drill started with us being put to bed one Sunday after lunch. Miss Martin had already told us what to expect; she told us that when we heard the bell and whistle together we were to treat the occasion like a real fire. This routine was practised often - initially we would be in our clothes and then gradually we progressed to being dressed in our nightwear – as it would be if there was a fire at night. When we were sent to our beds we did not know when we would hear the bell and whistle, Miss Martin didn't say.

One girl in our dormitory fell asleep and I remember feeling a little tired too but I forced myself to stay awake. It was well over half an hour after we had been put to bed that we heard the bell and whistle sound together. We all jumped out of bed, made sure the girl who had fallen asleep was woken, put our dressing gowns and slippers on and, as we had been told, placed a towel behind the bedroom door to let the firemen know that this room had no children left in it. It was the job of the oldest girl in the dormitory to make sure everybody was out safely.

We all went down the fire escapes and met in our playing field to be counted. When Miss Martin told us we had evacuated the building in four minutes we were all very pleased with ourselves. She also told us that we would be doing it all again next weekend with the firemen from Gullane Training School and we would see Mackie using her new chair hoist.

Next weekend arrived and the fire drill was repeated just as before – in under four minutes this time. The firemen were waiting in our playing field and gave us a good clap. We all then went to the front of the house to watch poor Mackie being shown how to use this strange contraption. She had to come out of her turret window and it was a good thing she was very slim. She was helped by one fireman from inside her bedroom and shown how to use the rope which would take her and the chair to the ground. We were all standing at the bottom willing her to come down safely. All we could hear was "Oh eck! Oh eck!" until her feet touched the ground. We all applauded her and at that point she turned to the fireman who had been helping her and said, "If there is ever a real fire at Tenterfield you had better come quick!" as she was not very keen on sitting on that seat again.

After all this excitement the firemen took the younger children up into the local hills in the fire engine – we could hear the bell ringing from Tenterfield. The older children were also taken for a ride too. Thankfully there was never a fire in Miss Martin's time but we still practised our drill faithfully.

7 Punishment

Our punishments were never severe, unlike some children who lived in care. If two children were fighting they would be sent to see Miss Martin who would ask them what had started the argument. The usual answer was "It was her" from each child, each blaming the other, to which Miss Martin would reply "Nothing will ever be sorted out with that kind of answer" and would tell the squabblers to sit and think of a much better answer than that. She would sit at her desk and carry on writing for what seemed like forever and she would then ask the children "Well, was it all worth while?" "No!" would come the reply. She would then ask the children in question to shake hands and to try and resolve their grievances in future without resorting to fighting as fighting solves nothing.

I remember once being sent to Miss Martin for being very, very rude. I think she was at the end of her tether with me at this time (and, unknown to me then, she was also ill), as she took her slipper out and began to bang the wall extremely hard with it, saying "You must stop being rude to my staff!" I could see how upset she was becoming and I began to cry, at which point she asked "Why are you crying?" My answer of "It's because you are getting very upset." brought the retort "Well, don't upset me again." I felt really bad and never spoke a wrong word to anybody after that.

As an adult myself now, I realise how much pain she must have been in, at the beginning of the illness from which she was not going to recover. Miss Martin and her staff would not allow swearing either. Their answer was that Tenterfield children did not swear because they always knew the proper word to use, and that using a swear word was just laziness as we all had the intelligence to use the 'proper word'. It was always said of Miss Martin's children that we could mix with the best as our manners and language skills were second to none.

8 Christmas Time

Rosalind, Grace and Evelyn in party dresses – made by Mrs Krumyre.

Every year, a few months before Christmas, Miss Martin would go down to the local dressmaking shop and pick out four patterns for Mrs Krumyre to make party dresses for the oldest girls at Tenterfield. After we had chosen our design we would then go and pick our material. I remember picking a really nice pale blue colour and I chose silver pump shoes to go along with the dress. (I notice that young girls are wearing pumps these days too...) Other girls chose yellow, green and pink and even the dress designs that we chose were all different.

The younger children all looked fantastic in their party dresses which would have been handed down from the older girls of previous years. The bigger boys would have been fitted with new suits and again the younger ones wore the hand-me-downs, which were all still as good as new as the party clothes were only used occasionally. We would all be looking very nice, hair done in ringlets which had to be done the night before for those who wanted them. The ringlets were created by using strips of rags and winding the hair round them – sleeping with the rags in was not too comfy!

Mrs Krumyre was absolutely first class when it came to making our party clothes. The girls would go into the sewing room for fittings and Miss Martin and the staff would not see the finished article until it was to Mrs Krumyre's satisfaction. When she was happy with her work we would all parade up to Miss Martin's room. We all thought we were models and Miss Martin would tell us how lovely we all looked.

Our piano was kept in the sewing room too. I managed to learn 'Chopsticks' but would have loved to have been able to play better, however it was not to be. The children would try and teach themselves and we were allowed to do this but were told never to bang at the ivories – not just for Mrs Krumyre's sake but for the piano's sake too. Before Christmas our piano always had to be tuned – I wonder why…

9 Christmas Eve And Christmas Day

Christmas Eve was a very happy time for all of us children. The staff had prepared all of the children's presents and put them in pillowcases with our names on them (I found this out when I got older). When I was younger it was Santa Claus who gave us gifts and as we got older we would keep it going for the younger ones – their excitement was infectious, trying to sleep on Christmas Eve was almost impossible but we would manage a few hours.

Uncle Willie (Lothian and Peebles Chief Constable), dressed as Santa Claus, would tiptoe around with Miss

Martin putting presents at the bottom of each child's bed, and in each child's clothes drawer he would place a brand new two and six (half crown) coin. This must have taken some time. I think he started around eleven o' clock and when he finished his delivery of presents he would be driven back to Edinburgh.

The children would be wakened by another child calling out "Santa has been!". This was usually around six o'clock in the morning but to Miss Martin and her staff this was a day for their children. Opening our presents was so exciting. There would be roller skates, books, board games, pencil-cases, a chocolate Santa for everyone, skipping ropes, cowboy dressing up sets,

Indian dressing up sets, paint books and paints and an orange and an apple. We were given things that were suited to each child's needs and capabilities.

Before breakfast we children would have eaten the chocolate Santas and fruit and be too busy playing with our new toys to worry about breakfast but Miss Martin would try and encourage us all to have something. After breakfast we would get dressed for church, and we found this time of year more enjoyable than a normal Sunday. We would enjoy singing all the carols and were told by the minister never to forget that there were children who were less fortunate than his parishioners and of course he was right.

After church it was home for lunch which was turkey (donated every year by a local farmer), roast potatoes, brussel sprouts, jelly and ice cream or Christmas pudding – this was the most popular of the puddings as there were silver sixpennies wrapped up in greaseproof paper in the pudding. We would have helped to put them into the pudding while it was being made, and all made a wish as we stirred it. We would have orange squash to drink and then after lunch we would prepare the dining room for our Christmas party.

This was a very exciting time for us all. The Christmas tree (which was also donated) looked splendid in the corner of our dining room, all decorated with fairy lights and our own homemade decorations with many presents under the tree for all the children. Some of these presents were given to the children by their foster aunts and uncles and those children who did not yet have foster aunts and uncles would still have the same amount of presents as those who did. This was arranged by Miss Martin so that no-one felt left out.

We would then start the party games. Our G.P. would play all the music for our games. One game we played was 'I sent a letter to my love', another was musical bumps, the Grand Old Duke of York and blind man's buff too along with many other games. Something which the older children took a bit more seriously was the display of Scottish country dancing which they performed for Miss Martin and all the adult guests.

After the party games we would all sit down and sing 'Jingle Bells', and in would come Santa (our G.P. or Uncle Willie – whoever was free at the time.) Opening our second set of presents was yet again a noisy event as you could imagine with sometimes over forty children opening their presents at the same time.   After all the paper was cleared away and our presents put aside in cupboards it was time to go into the playroom where all the tables were set for our party tea – scones, cakes, sandwiches, sausage rolls and of course our homemade Christmas cake and more orange squash.

At the end of the party all our guests were thanked for all the work they had put in and waved off. We would change out of our party clothes and into our play clothes and play with our presents once again. We were all in bed early that night with Miss Martin and the staff retreating exhausted to their rooms, but happy with the day's events.

10 "Uncle Willie"

'Uncle Willie' on the beach.

Willie Merrilees was the Chief Constable of Lothian and Peebles Constabulary and did a huge amount for the children at Tenterfield, not only playing the part of Santa Claus. He organised visits for us to the Edinburgh Military Tattoo, pantomimes at the theatre or on ice, and the circus when it came to Edinburgh. When the film *Greyfriar's Bobby* was being filmed in Edinburgh Uncle Willie came to Tenterfield with Bobby the dog and two of the actors to meet us all – Alex MacKenzie and the famous Gordon Jackson, but being children all eyes and hands were on Bobby - he really was a lovely wee dog.

We also met Roy Rogers, the American film star, via Uncle Willie. Roy threw a huge party in Edinburgh for many children from children's homes and I was fortunate enough to be one of them. We used to watch him on our black and white television. I remember asking him where Trigger was and he told me that poor Trigger had been shot in the leg while he was helping the Indians, and the vet in America had told him not to let Trigger travel but to let all the children know that Trigger was doing very well, and that on Roy's return he would be able to take him home. Of course being children and never having travelled abroad we accepted this as a very good explanation as to why Trigger was not with Roy!

When Uncle Willie organised the matinee for the Military Tattoo there would be many children from other homes there also. I always remember my last visit to the Tattoo with Tenterfield. The military bands were playing Chuck Berry's 'Let's Twist Again' and the commentator announced

Uncle Willie organising a sing-song

that all the children could enter the arena and twist the afternoon away. We all looked at Miss Martin and of course she said yes. When we returned to our seats she was sitting with the biggest smile on her face – yet again we were allowed to be children, she was always proud of her family.

On the way home we chatted all about the day's events. I have been back to the Tattoo since my childhood and when I sit waiting for it to begin I always think back to my visits there with my very large family from Tenterfield – what a lot of happy memories. 'Uncle Willie' made all this happen and to this day I think of him fondly and with much gratitude.

11 Mr McLaren The Gardener

Mr McLaren locking the greenhouse!

Mr McLaren, his wife and children lived in a tied cottage beside our field at Tenterfield. He always gave me the impression that he very much enjoyed his work. The front garden had a circular lawn which held a bed of the most beautifully coloured flowers. He planted arrangements for many special occasions. When it was the Queen's Coronation Mr McLaren had a crown of golden flowers planted with blue flowers either side arranged in the letters ER.

The windows at the front of Tenterfield always looked beautiful too with their blue window boxes full of red, white and blue flowers. To the right of the house at the front was our vegetable garden. We grew all our vegetables ourselves at Tenterfield and us children would go and collect carrots, leeks and potatoes for the cook – Mrs Hall. It was always nice to see the vegetables which you may have helped plant being turned into soup or mashed potatoes!

My brother Angus, along with some of the older boys, spent many an evening or weekend if necessary helping Mr McLaren and he tells me he felt he learned an awful lot about gardening from him. We were always allowed to help the gardener as long as in Miss Martin's words "He didn't mind". We also had our own orchard and many of the children would help with the fruit picking and Angus also learned how to graft fruit from Mr McLaren.

He was not only our gardener but the person who would repair our bikes when the chain came off or needed oiled, and he was also always ready to have fun with us too. I remember one very hot day he asked Mackie if it was alright to turn the hose on all of us children. We all ran inside and changed into our swimming costumes and then out into the courtyard – what fun we had. Miss Martin came out to see what all the laughter was about and by this time the courtyard resembled a swimming pool. The fun we had on days like that stays with me still.

At the rear of the house stood our greenhouse, which was detached from the main house. In my memories it looked Victorian but could have been from an earlier era. Mr McLaren grew all his plants from seed here. On one occasion I just happened to be passing the greenhouse when I noticed the door was unlocked. The tomatoes just looked so inviting so in I went and picked one. How juicy it was! He actually began to tell me to wash it first but too late, it was gone! I never found the greenhouse unlocked again...

Our field was always cut by a tractor and when this happened Mr McLaren would be on hand to make sure that we children were kept safely away from danger. We would sit on the fence surrounding the field, eagerly watching the grass being cut, ready to build our grass houses. We used to construct walls of grass with an opening on one side which was the doorway. We pretended these were houses although we were never able to put a roof on them! Another of his tasks was to set out our fireworks display with Miss Martin's help. We were never allowed near the fireworks but we would all help to build the bonfire and make the guy. He also became the father-figure that most of the children, myself included, did not have, and was a very well respected member of the community.

Sometimes Mrs McLaren would make tea and cakes for us when we had a break from building the bonfire. She was not employed by Tenterfield but we saw a lot of her too and she, like her husband, was also a very nice person.

12 Bonfire Night

Our celebrations were always held on the nearest Saturday to the 5th of November and while the bonfire was burning away we would throw potatoes into the bottom of the fire to bake. As this took a long time a member of staff would have been busy frying up sausages in the kitchen.

Another staff member would be in the pavilion having hung sticky, syrup covered apples from the ceiling for us to try and bite. Scones baked by Mrs Hall would have been dipped in treacle and hung from the ceiling too. Then it would be time for 'dooking'. This too was great fun and there was always someone prepared to give you a hand to catch the apple which always seemed to be move round and round the basin.

When it came time for the staff to take a turn 'dooking' it was the perfect opportunity for the children to get their own back! Mackie always said she thought we were trying to drown her but she and the other members of staff took it in good spirits. The children would spin the apples in the water to make it harder for the staff to catch one.

Fireworks would have already been setup in our field by Miss Martin and Mr McLaren. Catherine wheels were safely nailed onto strong pieces of wood which were hammered into the ground, rockets were dotted around the field in large jam jars and the children would be offered sparklers. Bangers would be set off too and I didn't like these very much I remember. Our bonfire night always went well and apart from the Tenterfield children, there would also be our school-friends and some of the domestic staff's children too. It was always a very enjoyable time for both children and staff and a good night was had by all.

13 Domestic Staff: Cook, Sewing Ladies and Laundry Lady

Our cook was Mrs Hall who had two assistants called Mrs Murray and Mrs Scobie. I spent many a time helping in the kitchen; we were allowed to go into the kitchen and offer our help as long as Mrs Hall agreed that we could. I remember being in the kitchen one day when Mrs Hall was preparing to make soup. She sent me to find Mr McLaren the gardener and ask him for twelve large carrots, turnips, onions and potatoes. I said to her "Why can't we have pea soup instead of vegetable?" to which she replied "I know that pea soup is your favourite but we must let the other children taste my vegetable soup as they have favourites too."

She was very fair-minded. She was a very, very good cook and made fantastic cakes and scones. We were allowed to help roll out the scone mixture and beat the cake mix and put it into the small cake trays. There was always a cake or scone for every child and member of staff. At Christmas time it was Mrs Hall who made the Christmas cake , fairy cakes, chocolate crispy cakes and all the other paraphernalia that went with any of our special days at Tenterfield. After all the cooking and baking Mrs Murray and Mrs Scobie would clean and scrub all the pots and baking utensils ready for their next use.

Whenever a child spent any time helping in the kitchen they would be unaware that they were learning while they enjoyed themselves. For example counting the twelve carrots for the soup, counting the eggs for the cake, weighing the flour and the sugar etc... We were also learning how to cook.

I was always told that one day I would be doing the same for my husband and family but would not need to use so many ingredients! I remember saying to Mrs Hall "But how will I manage to scale things down?" and the next time I went to help she had all the ingredients in one bowl to make cakes for the children and she gave me a separate bowl to make cakes for the staff; in this way I was able to learn to bake for smaller numbers of people. I enjoy baking but I don't do as much as I would like as I have a husband who will never wait for the cake to cool down! After the cake baking Mrs Hall, Mrs Murray, Mrs Scobie and myself would sit down to a cup of tea and a cake or hot scone (I loved the scones).

There was a day when I found myself in the kitchen on my own and decided to try tasting some of the foodstuffs in the cupboard. There was quite a lot of dried fruit so I had a little taste of that then some jelly crystals which were not too bad. At the bottom of the cupboard there were some very large bottles of vinegar so I had a little sip of that too. All this was done when the kitchen staff had just left to go home for the evening. I became quite fond of the taste of vinegar and continued to secretly have a sip until the time Miss Martin walked in and caught me. Firstly I was given a row for drinking the vinegar, then told what it would do to my insides and the ultimate punishment was to be told that I was not allowed to help in the kitchen or even go near it for four weeks. For many years I still had the urge to pick up a vinegar bottle when I saw one but I've got over it now! Miss Martin's words rang in my ears for a long time afterwards and the hardest part was not being allowed in the kitchen for so long as I loved helping.

Mrs Keating and Mrs Woods were in charge of looking after the large front hall, the front and back stairs and the bedrooms (which the children tidied for them). We made our own beds and put our mats on the bottom of the beds to make it easier for them to clean the floors. They also cleaned the back corridor and then into the downstairs toilets, the boot room and the bathrooms. Again we were expected to make things easier for them by hanging our face towels and toilet bags on our pegs.

I remember once coming in while Mrs Keating was mopping by the back door. She didn't raise her voice about a child running over her clean floor, only said "Be very careful as you might slip and hurt yourself." She had a very pleasant manner and a lovely soft voice and it was obvious that she loved her work.

Mrs Dunn, our laundry lady also looked happy at her work. The only time she would be slightly annoyed was when some child or member of staff did not put the irons or ironing board back in their rightful place. The Laundry was her domain but we used to help her carry out the wet washing for her to hang on the washing lines – 'her' washing green as it was known as. She did all the laundry for the children and Miss Martin, the staff did their own. Like Mrs Murray and Mrs Scobie, Mrs Dunn also had the most modern equipment in the laundry which made life easier for her too. When she had hung up all the freshly washed white sheets we would run straight through them and woe betide anyone who was caught…. There would be a lecture from her and Miss Martin. We soon stopped this as the fun we had was not worth the lectures we received afterwards, but Mrs Dunn ensured all the children's clothes were spotless!

When we were older Susan and I asked Miss Martin if we could do our own washing on one occasion. This was fine with her but she reminded us that Mrs Dunn liked all her equipment put back in its proper place. We both assured Miss Martin we would make sure this was done and got to work. First we used the washing machine, then the spin dryer and finally hung our clothes out to dry in the wind. When they were dry we took our clothes back to the laundry and ironed them. It seemed to take longer to put everything back in its rightful place than it had to do our washing, however next morning no comment was made so we must have put everything away properly which was a relief to Susan and I.

Every Friday night we would collect all our dirty washing and put it in the corner of our bathrooms, Miss Martin included, and then help Mackie or another member of staff to sort all the washing into separate piles of whites, coloureds, woollens etc… I was helping one Friday night when I asked Mackie which pile I should put Miss Martin's bloomers in. I was holding them against me and doing a little dance when suddenly I felt a tap on my shoulder – yes, it was Miss Martin, laughing along with everyone else around, telling me that it would be some time before I fitted into her bloomers. Another wave of laughter rolled around – I think it was the word 'bloomers' that did it. After all the hilarity we would carry the bundles of washing over to the laundry ready for Mrs Dunn on Monday morning.

I never asked where Mrs Krumyre came from but she was a very talented seamstress and was able to repair any article of clothing that needed repaired.

Alongside making our beautiful party dresses at Christmas she taught us to darn using a wooden toadstool and how to sew on buttons and fasteners in her spare time. The younger children would go and see her as she collected all the old cotton reels for them. She would give them a piece of wool and let them thread it through the reels. She would knot it for them and they would go off delighted with their homemade necklaces.

As I have already said the piano was kept in her sewing room and while I played 'Chopsticks' she would sew away quite happily. There didn't seem to be a sewing job that she couldn't tackle and when I was in high school my sewing skills were remarked upon which was all thanks to Mrs Krumyre.

14 Hens

I remember a time when we kept hens at Tenterfield. We had a chicken run with many hens and the only time I went to feed them they all ran at me as soon as I entered the run. I was terrified and just took off leaving them to help themselves to their food! I am still not too keen on birds to this day. Our gardener, along with some of the boys, would move the run every so often to keep the hens on fresh grass and I never volunteered to help. Mind you, I always liked hearing the cockerel crow in the morning. The hens did not stay too long at Tenterfield but I have no idea why Miss Martin stopped keeping them.

Perhaps there were other children like me who were frightened of them.

15 Council Inspections Of Tenterfield

Tenterfield was inspected on a regular basis by the council who put their findings in a ledger which was held by Miss Martin at Tenterfield. I managed to gain access to the ledger and example entries follow below. Unfortunately the dates for these entries were obscured but they still serve as proof of how well Tenterfield was run.

1. Evening visit: younger children in bed in a nice, clean and safe environment. Some older children in the playroom dancing to the music of Buddy Holly and Scottish country dancing. There

were more children still outside playing in their field.

2. Afternoon visit: House very clean and tidy as usual. The children were playing outside, the older ones at school.

3. Start of school holidays: children very excited about going their camp.

4. Easter week: Older children decorating their hard-boiled eggs.

5. Christmas Week: Children very busy getting ready making Christmas decorations.

6. Additional: The house is very clean and tidy which is thanks to the domestic staff; kitchen spotless, all other areas of the

house – bedrooms, bathrooms and cupboards very neat and tidy.

#All these quotes were signed and the inspections were always unannounced which I think was the best way for it to be done, especially when there was nothing to hide.

16 Harvest Thanksgiving

Once a year we had a harvest thanksgiving at church. After the church service our minister always gave the job of taking the basket of fruit and vegetables up to Hermandflat hospital. This hospital was specifically for adults with learning disabilities and as a child I was terrified of them. I hated the job but was always chosen and never thought to object – we always did as we were asked in those days. I used to ring the bell and run, having put the basket at the door. I would run all the way home and still wonder if that was the reason I became such a fast runner.

Often when we were being taken out for a walk we would meet the adults from the hospital coming the other way, being taken out too. As children these adults frightened us, as we did not understand about their disabilities but if any of Miss Martin's children made fun of them then their disabilities would be explained to us the minute we arrived home.

17 **Mr Todrick, Our Neighbour**

Mr Todrick was our neighbour who was deaf and dumb. His orchard trees reached the top of our wall which was low on our side meaning we didn't even have to stretch very far to reach his apples. Although we had an orchard of our own it was more fun to pinch his apples.

As he could not shout at us he would fire his shotgun in the air to warn us off and we would scarper in different directions. Shortly after this he would appear at our front door with a note for Miss Martin detailing our misdemeanours. When this happened Miss Martin would then remind us at the next mealtime why we were not to steal his, or anyone else's apples. We were told if they fell off his trees into our garden then we could take them so from then on we would shake the branches of his tree until they fell into our garden. I'm sure that his method of scaring us away from his trees would not be allowed these days!

18 Miss Cooper And Granny Millar

Miss Cooper was a friend of Miss Martin's and soon became a friend to all the children too. She was an excellent golfer, in fact although I am not certain, she may have been a champion lady golfer in her time. She asked Miss Martin if she could teach us to play golf one summer.

We happened to be holidaying in Gullane that year as the campsite at Lady Haddington's estate was waterlogged. We were staying in Gullane primary school and directly opposite the school was a golf course. As I was a hockey player she seemed to think I would make a good golfer but I'm afraid at that time of my life it was not to be. Hockey players did not lift their sticks above their heads and she just could not teach me at all as I would not raise the club properly! I have played golf since on a nine hole course and managed to get a hole in one, only once, but obviously some of her teaching had rubbed off on me. The boys seemed to be much better golfers than the girls to me...

Miss Cooper had a Dalmatian called Roger and he spent many a time at our house with our dog in the field. He too was a very happy dog, barking joyfully as he ran around our field chasing sticks or balls. Miss Cooper was very well spoken too, both she and Miss Martin had been friends for many years and they must have been very good friends indeed as while researching for this book I discovered Miss Martin's will and in it Miss Cooper was named as executor. We children did not have much to do with Miss Cooper but we always had plenty to do with Roger the dog! I visited Mackie recently and she told me that she always thought that Miss Cooper's dog was called 'Rajah' as her accent was so posh. She roared with laughter when she realised that the dog's name was actually Roger…

Granny Millar with one of our dogs

Granny Millar was a lovely old lady who had been a friend of Miss Martin's mother. She often came to visit us but I never discovered whether she had been married or had a family although she certainly understood children very well. I sometimes heard her say to Miss Martin "Oh! Just let them be children."

just like a grandmother would say. She had a lovely smile and I remember her as not being very tall and how she liked it very much when we called her Granny Millar. At the front of Tenterfield we had a dell which we were not allowed to go into for safety reasons, mainly because it was at the front of the house.

Granny Millar knew this rule as well as the children and staff. On one of Miss Martin's days off she was driving with Granny Millar past Tenterfield when Granny Millar noticed some children in the dell. They were with a member of staff, probably Mackie, who was showing them the blanket of snowdrops and crocuses covering the dell. On seeing this Granny Millar rolled the car window down and shouted "Liberty for the children!" - she had a great sense of humour and would do this whenever she saw us in the dell.

19 John White Footballer
(Tottenham Hotspur)

One Saturday evening after tea we were visited by a young man who amazed us all by the way he could control a ball with his feet. The boys and the girls all joined in trying to mimic his 'keepy-uppy' skills; he was really talented at this and one of the boys said to him that he should really join a football team to which he replied that he was already in a team called Tottenham Hotspur. None of us children recognised the name at the time, only that it was not a Scottish team.

After playing football for a while with us in our field he told us it was an

English team and every Saturday after that Miss Martin would tell us what number he was wearing and we would cheer him on if the game was on television. John White was the footballer's name and he came from Musselburgh, a small town not far from Haddington. Presumably Miss Martin had asked him to visit, we never knew, but we were all saddened when we heard that he had died as he had made us very happy. He was struck and killed by lightning while playing golf in 1964.

20 Foster Aunts and Uncles

When some of the Tenterfield children reached a certain age (usually twelve or thirteen), they were given a foster Aunt and Uncle. My foster Aunt and Uncle were called Sally and Vic. They had two boys who were younger than me. The elder boy was called Gordon and the younger one was Allan.

I began by visiting them on a Sunday after lunch for a few hours and then it was extended for longer. When Miss Martin was satisfied that the family and children were suited to each other and were settled she would allow the children to stay overnight with their foster family. Uncle Vic was the local Bank Manager in a little town called

Newtongrange, and Aunt Sally was Commissioner for the Girl Guides. She was also a fantastic baker just like her mother had been. I loved going to visit them but it felt strange at first going to a much smaller house and having my own bedroom. Later in life Aunt Sally told me that she was very worried about me not eating when I came to visit them at first. The real reason I was so shy was that the cakes looked so good that I really wanted to try them all but my manners wouldn't allow me to, so I just waited until I was asked if I would like one.

It didn't seem long to me before I settled into their family home. I would stay with them for weekends if I was not playing sport. In the summer when they came to collect me we would go for a drive before going to their house; sometimes it would be North Berwick, sometimes a drive in the countryside. By then I really felt part of the family – the little girl they had never had. When I met Aunt Sally's family I was asked if I minded being called 'wee Margaret' as Aunt Sally's sister was called Margaret too – I didn't mind at all, it made me feel like an individual and quite special, so from then on I was always known to Aunt Sally and Uncle Vic's families as 'wee Margaret'.

Some Sundays I would go with them to visit Gordon and Allan's grandparents. In the beginning I would stand back when Gordon and Allan were given pocket money by their grandparents as I didn't want to impose on their family life, but as soon as their grandparents saw my face I was told to come and get my pocket money too. They told me "When you come to visit with Sally and Vic you are one of the family too.", and from then on I was really happy.

I learned a lot from them, especially how a small family lived in comparison to my large one at Tenterfield and was often invited to their grandchildren's birthday parties. After spending my weekends there I was driven back to Tenterfield by Uncle Vic and the boys and Aunt Sally always came too. They always had problems getting the boys to leave as they would go off to play in our field dressed in their Sunday best. I always felt sad when they went back to their own house but Miss Martin would reassure me that they were very good people and would come back for me again and of course they did.

As I was growing up they played a very large part in my life. It was Aunty Sally I first turned to when I was getting married and again when Miss Martin died. When I received the news that Miss Martin had died I was devastated; I had no-one to turn to apart from my husband who did his very best but it was not quite the same as the comfort I got from Aunt Sally. She had a way with words and a very sympathetic nature and as I poured my heart out to Aunt Sally she comforted me and helped me through what was a very difficult time for me. This special, loving family was truly remarkable and I was very fortunate to have been introduced to them by Miss Martin. I will always remember them with much love and fondness.

21 Leaving Home

When I was about fifteen years old Miss Sinclair (the Welfare Officer from Edinburgh) brought a woman to see me. I was told that this person was my mother. I had stopped asking Miss Martin about my life before Tenterfield a long time ago and had just presumed my mother had died but here she was all happy and smiling, handing me a fistful of money, telling me that she was my mother and would just love to have me home. I was furious and said to her "You want me home? I am home and I certainly do not want to be paid to go and stay with you!"

I actually felt nothing but disgust. I came out of the office having only spent five minutes in her company and told Miss Sinclair "That woman wants me to go and stay with her and says she is my mother – No thank you I said!" As I did not want to live with my mother it was arranged that I would live in a hostel in a small town called Gorebridge, almost midway between Haddington and Edinburgh. Children were only allowed to stay in Tenterfield until they were sixteen and the hostel was a sort of halfway house for girls who had been in care and were about to go out into the big world and work and look after themselves. As a result of this I was in care until the age of eighteen.

Miss Martin was puzzled when I rejected my birth mother but I told her that she, with the help of her staff and the ever-growing family at Tenterfield, had given me more than I could have ever wished for. I was taught values which seem to be lacking at times today – respect for yourself, others, the elderly, to always remember my manners. Miss Martin knew her children could go anywhere in the world and be very proud of their upbringing as I was and still am.

Miss Martin took me into Edinburgh to buy all my clothes in preparation for leaving Tenterfield. I received my first pair of high-heeled shoes then, lots of underwear, dresses, nylons, a winter coat, a summer coat, cardigans, jumpers, toiletries, dressing gown and nightwear. I chose the clothes myself and also was given a very large suitcase to put all my things in which eased the pain of leaving home slightly.

My last night at Tenterfield was awful. I cried my eyes out with Miss Martin trying to console me and doing her best not to break down too. She told me that Tenterfield was, and always would be, my home but that I must allow other children to be brought up in the same way I was, and be given the chance of a better life. She was right but it was a very difficult thing to do, to leave Tenterfield. For myself and all the other children who had the good fortune to have had Miss Martin to guide us, nurture us, teach us right from wrong, and so many other little things, I will always be eternally grateful.

22 The Hostel

The hostel, situated in Gorebridge, was such a small house compared to what I was used to that it took me some time to settle in. The couple who ran it – Mr and Mrs Brown – were extremely nice people and I was welcomed into the fold. There were five other girls living there too, from other children's homes, all out working. Some worked in the nearby Border towns in the mills but this was not for me. I was given plenty of time to settle in and make the transition from child to young adult.

I was probably given about three months from what I remember and then Mrs Brown asked me what type of job I would like to do. I just blurted out "To look after children who have no father or mother." I thought I was beginning to sound just like Miss Martin but I truly felt that this was to become my vocation. (Those people who know me now, forty-five years later, would probably agree). Mrs Brown, with the help of Mrs Sinclair managed to get me a place with the Royal Scottish Society for Prevention of Cruelty to Children (RSSPCC) which was quite ironic really as that is where I had first been dealt with as a child many years before, only the address had changed.

Before I began work there, while I still lived at the hostel, I was taking the Brown's dog Mac for a walk as I often did. A painter and decorator wolf whistled at me which I thought was 'rather common' and ignored.

I forgot all about him until it happened again the next time I was walking the dog. This time the young man spoke to me and asked why the dog only had three legs. I couldn't answer this as I had never asked the Browns why myself; however he then went on to ask me out. I was a bit worried about this but after having taken advice from Mr Brown we arranged a time to meet. The only draw back was that he lived in Portobello – not very near Gorebridge when you had to travel by bus – but it worked out ok. Our first date was in Princes Street in Edinburgh and I was late... The next time I was to meet him in town and I didn't turn up at all! Mr and Mrs Brown were going to see the opening of the new Forth Road Bridge and had asked me if I would like to come along and I did. I was not too happy about letting Gordon down and at the back of my mind I could hear Miss Martin saying "Margaret! That is no way to treat people!" but I also knew I would never have the opportunity to see the opening of the bridge again.

Thankfully Gordon forgave me and we made time for each other from then on. After I had been seeing Gordon for three years Miss Martin thought it was time to meet Gordon. I remember thinking to myself as I was on my way to tell him about Miss Martin, "What if he says no?" Thankfully he was quite happy to come and meet her. She had the knack of making people feel at ease and Gordon thought that she was a concerned Mother figure who only wanted the best for her children. Luckily for me he passed her test; she told me afterwards that she thought he would take care of me and he even spoke very nicely!! She wished us both well. I always felt quite sad that Miss Martin never married but I know for a fact she would not have changed her life for anybody.

23 Children Who Came And Went.

I could never understand why some children came to Tenterfield for a while and then returned home – I seemed to have stayed there forever. One family came to Tenterfield when their mother died as their father was unable to look after them and work too. There was Marion, Andrew and David whose nickname was 'Ginger' as he had red hair.

Miss Martin met the new family and their father stayed a while until they settled in. Before he left he was asked to do his best to visit his children at weekends if his shifts allowed it (he was a miner), and he did this. After a few years their father announced that he was going to be married again and his new wife was quite happy to have his children back with them and she would do her best for them. I remember feeling sad when Marion left, she was a great girl and I would miss her. I still wondered why it was that some children came and went and I stayed, but she was to return...

Almost two and a half years later Marion, Andrew and David returned to Tenterfield. Their father had been killed in a pit accident and they were devastated and really very sad. They were all younger than me and I felt so sorry for them, but after they had settled in again they seemed to cheer up a little. Only recently I was speaking to Marion and she told me the story behind their return to Tenterfield. When their dad died the Welfare Officer, Miss Sinclair was called in by their stepmother. Miss Sinclair sat the children down and asked the children where they would like to live now their father was dead. She told them that their natural Aunt and Uncle, who lived in Fife, would be happy to take care of them but they said to Miss Sinclair "Please can we go back to Tenterfield as we were all happy there", and that was what happened, they returned to their friends in Tenterfield.

Another child I remember only staying for a short while was a girl called Brenda who was deaf and dumb. I remember sitting in the playroom with some other children and Brenda was teaching us how to sign the alphabet. She wasn't there for long but long enough to teach us sign language.

24 Clothes

When winter came we would all be fitted for our 'best' clothes (for wearing on Sundays). Green Harris tweed coats were made for the girls, blue for the boys, and they kept us really warm. Girls also wore differently coloured gingham dresses and a navy cardigan while the boys, depending on their age, wore either short trousers and a jacket or long trousers, jacket, shirt and tie. We also wore our best shoes on Sundays and berets for the girls, caps for the boys. We were well clad in those days…

When we arrived home from church we changed into the clothes we loved best – our play clothes. In these clothes we were given the freedom to be children (something that children today seem to miss out on). We were allowed to climb trees in our play clothes, play in the grass cuttings when the grass had been cut, dig in the mud and get dirty and sledge in winter or climb the hills near Tenterfield. I remember coming home from a walk in the hills with my clothes definitely not as clean as they had been when I left but nothing was ever said. This is why they were called our play clothes, we didn't have to worry about being messy in them, we could do what children do best – play!

When summer arrived our play clothes were shorts and t-shirts, sandals and bare feet – no socks! We would be ready for any adventure – some of us used to go down to the river Tyne and swim, accompanied by a member of staff who would be in charge of all the towels and our dry clothes. We were only allowed in the river if we were swimming, the children who couldn't or didn't want to could play in the water pools dotted about or in the very shallow part of the river. Only a few children did this at one time - for safety reasons we could not all go together – those who didn't come swimming would go for a bike ride or even just enjoy the peace in the house when most of us were out. Both boys and girls wore school uniform Monday to Friday. I loved wearing mine which some of the other children found strange, mainly the new ones and the older children. One older girl didn't like wearing hers as we all wore the same uniform whereas our play clothes were all completely different, no two articles the same, even our play shoes and sandals were different.

We were always given the best footwear too; 'Clarks' for best which were then relegated to play shoes when they got a bit tattered. I hope I passed on the importance of play to my own family along with the knowledge that clothes can be washed and mended if torn but you only have one childhood, and thank goodness I had the one that I had.

25 Boats

We children were invited for a boat trip around the Bass Rock and to visit the lighthouse and climb to its top. I remember that all the children who were going had to line up for our sea sickness pills which, I have to say, at least kept some of us from being sick! All aboard the big boat (to us), and off we sailed, not all of the children, only the older ones – about fifteen to twenty of us along with Miss Martin and Mackie.

We arrived at the Bass Rock, having sailed round it twice, ready to climb up to the lighthouse. We could only do so a few at a time but the view was spectacular and we spent about an hour on the Rock. On our descent from the lighthouse it seemed to be a bit trickier getting back on to the boat but we all made it safely. When we arrived back on dry land our bus was waiting to take us home. What an exciting day we had had, we couldn't wait to tell our friends at school on Monday morning what we had done.

On another occasion we had the opportunity to go out with the North Berwick fishing fleet. I remember this trip only because we had to get up very, very early, around two o'clock in the morning. I didn't mind as I was excited to be on a boat again. When we left shore I felt fine but the sea was obviously choppier than our last trip with the waves making the boat rise and fall quite dramatically (I felt). Even having taken a sea sickness pill I felt really nauseous and I just could not wait to reach dry land again. I never went on another boat trip again, even although many other children continued on these trips for as long as Miss Martin was at Tenterfield.

26 Mother's Day

Mother's Day was a very special day for Miss Martin. She would have a long lie in bed, at least until it was time to get ready for church. We would all sing 'Happy Mother's Day to You!' to the tune of 'Happy Birthday'. After her late breakfast we would all go to church and when our minister wished all the mothers present a happy Mother's day he would also wish Miss Martin one too and her face would be beaming with pride. We also made her birthday a special day and I discovered later in life that she had kept all the birthday and Mother's day cards that I had given her and I now have these back.

Our handmade card

FROM ALL the children

Sylvia,
Jenny,
Emily,
Grace,
Alison,
Julia
Mary
Irene
Janet
Rose
Valerie
Sammy C.
Sammy K.
Paul
Jane
Kenneth
Heather
Ingilia
Prastica
Baby Ian.

Bettk·
Joyce,
And from all the
boys. xxvixxxxxxxx x

Signed by some of the children

172

27 Susan and Dennis' Wedding

Miss Martin, Gordon (Uncle Vic's son), Dennis, Susan, Dennis' mum and Uncle Vic

Susan and Dennis became engaged in December nineteen sixty two, having known each other for three years. Susan still came home to Tenterfield when she had time off work like so many of Miss Martin's children. Dennis asked Miss Martin's permission to marry Susan and she gave it. Susan and Dennis had arranged their own wedding, deciding on the place they were getting married, the time and where the reception was to be held. They sent invitations to the staff at Tenterfield, some of the children and Miss Martin of course. Miss Martin replied saying she was quite disappointed that Susan and Dennis were not being married in the 'family' church, that is the West Church in Haddington. Susan and Dennis had chosen a registry office wedding as it was the cheaper option in those days.

Around this time Miss Martin had a short spell in hospital but thankfully for Susan and the Tenterfield children she was back on her feet quite quickly and serious discussion was taking place regarding 'the' wedding. Miss Martin convinced Susan and Dennis to be married from the 'family' church and to hold their reception at Tenterfield. They were so delighted at her wishes that they hastily cancelled all their original plans and although Miss Martin made sure they had time to think things over they did not have to think twice before accepting.

As Susan had already bought a suit for the Registry Office wedding she now had to try and find a white wedding dress, organise flowers, a cake, ushers and she was determined that she would. I had by this time a foster auntie and uncle who were often at Tenterfield and who became very good friends of Miss Martin and her evergrowing family.

Well, as luck would have it Auntie Sally's sister had been married only a few weeks previously and Aunt Sally asked her if she would mind Susan borrowing her dress. Her reply was that as long as Susan didn't mind a second-hand dress she would be delighted to give it to her. She was also given the veil too. The dress had to be altered slightly and this was done by Mrs Krumyre. The cake was donated by a local baker, flowers from the local florist, almost everything was arranged apart from who would give the bride away. Susan asked Uncle Vic if he would do the honours and he was delighted. Having two boys of his own he was the perfect father figure for the task.

All the wedding gifts were displayed in Miss Martin's sitting room a few nights before the wedding and in the age old tradition Susan and her bridesmaid stayed overnight at Tenterfield the night before the wedding. A wedding day, as we all know, is a very busy time and this one was even more so, taking place in a children's home which was unheard of at the time. All the younger children had to be given breakfast and the older ones too but the excitement was running very high. The reception was being held in the dining room between four and five o' clock in the afternoon and so the children had to be given their tea that day in the playroom meaning that room too had to be rearranged but all went well on the day. Mrs Hall prepared the three course meal for the guests as well as cooking for the children as usual. There was a toast of whisky for the men and sherry for the ladies.

Miss Martin looked really happy and proud of the whole event and how the day had turned out. Looking at the wedding photos she certainly looked like the mother of the bride. Susan will always remember her wedding day as in her own words 'It was really extra special!' After the wedding Susan and Dennis changed for their honeymoon which was a fortnight touring the Trossachs and they are still married to this day – forty six years on.

28 My Wedding To Gordon

Gordon and I

(not as happy as we should have been).

Gordon and I married on the eleventh of June nineteen sixty six at Portobello Old Parish Church. Gordon had to meet Miss Martin for her approval and I remember thinking to myself on the bus on the way to Haddington – 'What if she doesn't like him?' When we arrived she asked him about his job and would he take good care of me. He said he would and we have been married for forty three years. My wedding was not like Susan's. I am not, and never will be, a wearer of frilly clothes – especially white.

Some time before our wedding, around the time of our engagement I took Gordon to meet my natural mother and everything seemed to go well. My natural mother had remarried, to a very nice Polish man who was always pleasant when we met. Gordon and I had set the date and everything was going to plan. My natural mother wanted to pay for it all – I wasn't too keen – in fact if I am honest I did not want her there at all. Aunt Sally and Uncle Vic were going to gift me my wedding but when Aunt Sally heard about my mother's offer she thought I should give her the chance to do this for me. She thought it may have been a way of atoning for the past as she had never been part of my life as I grew up. I agreed on one condition – Uncle Vic would give me away. My Aunt Sally was always available when I needed advice which was truly welcomed.

Almost three weeks before my wedding I went to visit my natural mother to see how the plans were coming along. She told me everything was going to plan but three days before I was due to be married the most awful thing which could happen to any bride-to-be happened. Her words were "What wedding are you talking about?" When I replied "Mine" she asked me if I expected her to pay. I reminded her that she had offered but she denied this. I left her house very angry and never returned to visit her again.

When I arrived back at my place of work I was able to make a phone call to Aunt Sally, crying my eyes out. When she had calmed me down I was able to tell her what my natural mother had said. So Aunty Sally and Uncle Vic rallied round to get my wedding day in motion. In three days they did wonders. The cake was being made, the food was on order, the drinks for the toast were in hand and their garden was looking fantastic for our reception. Then my big day arrived. I wore a lovely pale blue dress (my favourite colour then), a cream coat which Aunt Sally bought and one of Aunt Sally's most famous hats. She had many; I did not really want to wear one but as we were being married in church I respected her wishes.

Uncle Vic drove me from their house at Bell's Mains, just outside Gorebridge, to the church. I felt we chatted just like father and daughter, he was reassuring me that he liked Gordon and he too felt that Gordon would take care of me. Arriving at the church I was really happy to see Miss Martin's smiling face waiting to wish us well along with Aunt Sally and Gordon's family.

After we became husband and wife the minister approached me to tell me that my natural mother was waiting outside at the front of the church apparently looking to cause a disturbance so we would have to leave by the back door. I was a bit unhappy about this but for the sake of peace we did. I had told the minister beforehand about the situation with my natural mother and thank goodness I did. Everyone who was important to me was waiting out the back for us. It took me years to realise why I looked so unhappy in one of my wedding photos but all became clear to me in the end. We all drove down to Aunt Sally and Uncle Vic's house where we had our reception outside in their garden. The weather was beautiful and I could not have asked for a better wedding or reception. Gordon and I were going on honeymoon to a caravan at Eddelston near Peebles. Uncle Vic drove us there and as I write this we have been married for forty three years.

29 My Brothers

My brothers Jimmy, Winston and Angus all joined the navy and their careers began with them going down south to join the HMS Ganges. Jimmy and Winston, who were older than Angus, joined first and when they came home with photos of their lives aboard the Ganges, Angus found their chats very interesting. One photo, for example, was of both Jimmy and Winston standing right at the top of the mast. Jimmy and Winston thought that seeing this might put Angus off wanting to join up but it didn't, and he soon joined up and served fourteen years.

Tommy, on the other hand, joined the army but he didn't seem to enjoy that as much as the others enjoyed the navy.

Tommy now lives in Thurso and moved there with his wife and children and no job to go to. Having always been taught by Miss Martin that you worked to support your family, he bought an ice-cream van and began selling ice-cream. After a while he felt that he did not want to spend his life selling ice-cream so he sold the van, bought a car and started a taxi business. This turned into a very viable business and Tommy has no regrets about moving so far away. It gives Angus (now retired) and myself a reason to visit when possible and we think the country is beautiful up there.

30 Fostering

During our early married life Gordon and I decided to foster children. We first began short-term fostering and were then asked to foster a little girl. This arrangement was initially to be short-term too, but she finally stayed with us for three and a half years. She was a lively and bubbly little girl who eventually went home happily to be with her mother. She is now forty years old and married with three girls of her own. We have kept in touch with her and when we speak with her she always tells us she has happy memories of her time spent with us.

After this little girl left us we were asked to foster three-year-old twins which we duly did. We were originally asked to look after them until their parents were capable of looking after the twins themselves. Sadly, this day never came, and when they were nine we were told that the twins were going to be put up for adoption. Gordon and I always believed that this decision should never have taken so long to be made.

During this adoption period the twins were still allowed to visit their natural parents while being fostered by ourselves. This situation was a very awkward one for us as every time they visited their parents they returned having forgotten everything we had taught them.

This was due to the fact there were no boundaries set for them by their parents who exercised no control over them.

Gordon and I had to make a decision regarding their adoption – would they go to a new family or stay with us? We both felt that it was cruel for them to begin a new life again with another family, having lived with us for so long. They were settled with us and happy, so we adopted them and they are now part of our family - both adults now and living their own lives. Their father is dead now but they still keep in touch with their natural mother too which we have always encouraged. We have discovered that this approach has worked very well for us all.

One of my main reasons for keeping contact with their natural parents was for the following reason: if, and when, health issues arose, the twins would know all about their family history and therefore would not be in the same position that I have found myself in, that is having no knowledge of my own family's medical background.

When their natural father died Colin asked us if his father's funeral cortege could leave from our house and if we would also hold his wake at our house. Of course we were pleased to do so and his natural mother also attended.

31 Josephine's Birthday Party

One of my foster children – Josephine – somehow managed to find us again after many, many years and invited us to her fortieth birthday party recently. Three of her sisters, whom we knew from their childhood days, were also there. They had been put into a children's home and we fostered Josephine.

Her mum used to visit us most weekends as she had a sister who lived near our home at the time. These visits went well, sometimes her mother would bring the sisters to visit Josephine which made our flat feel very crowded as it was not big enough to hold so many people, but for Josephine it was all worthwhile.

On meeting the girls again I felt that their lives seemed to be a bit better than they had been in the past, but Josephine seems to have fared the best, being both lovely and caring as is her husband. Josephine also gave me the impression of being a very caring Mum and their three girls too were very happy.

Josephine told me that when she left us to return home to her mother and begin school when she was five, her mother was often not at home when she came back from school. She had to sit in a very cold stairway until six o'clock when her mother would return. It wasn't that her mother worked, Josephine thinks that she was just forgotten about and she has held that memory with her all these years.

At the party Josephine introduced us to her mother-in-law and all her friends, some of whom had never known until now that she had been fostered, and we were introduced to everyone as her foster mum and dad. She also said 'I will not lose touch with you two again' – her words not mine, and we are very happy to keep in touch with her too. Her sisters also asked me at the party why I had not fostered them too, but they were older and had had a very difficult childhood. Because Josephine was the youngest she was sent to us so that she would not have to go through the trauma her elder sisters had experienced.

Things have turned out well all round for Josephine's own family. She told me that on the Sunday after her party, weather permitting, she was planning to abseil down the side of the Forth Bridge for charity of course. We are very proud of our own children and seeing Josephine now, how she has turned out after the start she had in life, we are also very proud of her too.

32 My Job

I have held several different jobs during my career, from being a nanny to becoming a nurse in Leith Hospital, but currently I work for Social Services as a day-carer, looking after babies and toddlers up to the age of three, whose mothers are having difficulty coping with young children. Depending on circumstance I can look after a child for one day a week up to four days each week from 08.30 to 14.30 daily.

I feel very much concerned for some of these children. In certain sections of society today it is common to hear parents cursing and swearing at their children with some parents seemingly incapable of speaking to their children, only shouting at them. I believe that many of these children will continue this negative life-cycle until it can be broken by intervention somehow, which is the purpose of my current job. These children are not taught right from wrong and do not respect their peers or others. They seem to be living in a society purely concerned with instant gratification and acquisition.

I also feel that these children dictate to their parents rather than being guided by them. I wonder, could it be that their parents have also had a lack of discipline and guidance in their own lives and don't know how to cope any other way? Sadly, perhaps it is the only way of life they know. In my opinion more government aid and intervention is needed to help these parents acquire the parenting skills they need while their children are at a vulnerable age, as I strongly feel that the early years of a child's development is the time when help is most necessary and also results are most successful. I know that with the children I care for they are happy once they settle with me. They accept my boundaries and when they leave my care, usually around the age of three to go into nursery education, I feel that I have given them a good start in their young lives. I firmly believe children are not born 'bad' but just need guidance and I would like to think that the good upbringing I received as a child has contributed to the knowledge and guidance I have passed on to 'my' parents and their children.

33 Children In Care Today

I sometimes feel saddened for children when I hear that foster placements have not worked out for a child for whatever reason, as I genuinely believe I was fortunate to have been given a very stable upbringing. I strongly believe that stability is the most important factor for children in care and personally, I never for one moment missed not having my natural parents around. Being in one place for my entire childhood until the age of sixteen gave me everything any child needs to have. I had stability, education, love and security – exactly what any parent wants for their child – as Miss Martin and her staff made sure that all of the children at

Tenterfield never missed out on all these things.

Maybe that is why I do the job I do today as I know exactly what it's like and I hope that I have helped pass on to the children and parents I look after, everything that was passed on to me by Miss Martin and her staff in Tenterfield. Some people may read this and have other opinions about Tenterfield but I know that this is how I felt about my life in care and I genuinely cannot recollect any memories of abuse or ill treatment of any kind while I lived at Tenterfield. I used to tell my own children that they would have enjoyed living at Tenterfield and when they were young I would visit Miss Martin there where instead of being my 'mum' she became the doting grandmother to my own children. She was a remarkable woman, as were her staff. We were brought up to never feel different because we lived in a children's home. Friends came for tea, on birthdays and also to stay with us as we sometimes stayed at friends' houses too, so, as you can see, 'sleepovers' are not a new thing, they happened all those years ago too.

My husband, who came from a family of nine children whose parents were not well off, has always said how fortunate I was to have been so well looked after and cared for as things were a lot tougher for his family.

34 Miss Martin's Obituary

(Obituary originally published in The Haddingtonshire Courier Dec 16th 1966)

The late Miss Dorothy Martin

Miss Dorothy Kathleen Martin who was 'mother' to hundreds of children during her 13 years as matron of Tenterfield Home, Haddington died in hospital on Monday.

Miss Martin's love for the children in her care was legendary far beyond East Lothian and her untimely death is a sad blow to the community in which she was so highly respected.

A small woman with a big heart, Miss Martin devoted her life to the care of children first as matron of Glasclune the Dr. Barnardo Home in North Berwick and later at Tenterfield.

It was a tribute to Miss Martin that long after they had left Tenterfield, many of her "children" returned, some for weekends, others to spend Army or Navy leave in the surroundings which she had made happy during their childhood.

A keen girl Guider, Miss Martin started a branch of the movement during her years at Glasclune and it was always her delight to take the children to camp at Tyninghame or drive them into the hills for a ramble or picnic. Her small figure striding up the streets of Haddington was more often than not distinguished by the children trotting around her.

Born in 1906 Miss Martin lived with her parents near Tunbridge Wells. Her father was a partner in the sports car manufacturing firm of Aston Martin and in the early days of motor racing was a familiar sight on the old Brooklands racing circuit outside London. It was after his death that Miss Martin moved North with her mother to set up home in North Berwick. After returning to the South for a short spell as matron of a small children's home, she returned to North Berwick as matron of Glasclune.

Although she had been in failing health for some years Miss Martin refused to give in until a few weeks ago when her illness forced her to go to Edinburgh Royal Infirmary. One of her last wishes was to be allowed to return to Tenterfield and her "family".

Miss Martin is not one who will be readily forgotten in Haddington for there are few such examples of selfless dedication to the service of others: and few women prepared to devote a lifetime seeking happiness for the children who most need it.

After the service at St. Baldrid's Church, which I attended along with some of Tenterfield's older children, we had a long walk behind the funeral car up to the cemetery to her well-earned resting place. Looking around me and seeing the many people in attendance made me proud to have been one of her children. When I hear the saying 'Blood is thicker than water' I have to say that I disagree and it certainly does not apply to me. When my natural mother died I had to be persuaded to go to her funeral by my older sister Nancy and I did, but only to keep the peace. This was the very first time that I sang 'The Lord's My Shepherd' all the way through, without a tear in my eye, at any funeral. Miss Martin was certainly a 'mother figure' to me, in fact she used to be known as 'Mother' to us all.

THE END

Appendix 1: Tenterfield House Ground Floor and Gardens

Our house was very large with many nooks and crannies. When you entered through the front door there was quite a large vestibule where there was a guest toilet and cloakroom. The door from here led into a very large hall. On your right was a beautiful marble fireplace with niche either side. One held a marble bust of a man (I'm not sure who he was), and the other always held a vase of cut flowers.

Opposite the fireplace there was a long, quite narrow table which held Miss Martin's father's trophies. The floor was covered in green linoleum, always highly polished. Halfway down the hall on the left was our playroom which was a good sized room to play in. Inside the playroom to the left there was a long row of pine cupboards which housed our books and toys. The large bay window in our playroom was covered in a very strong wire mesh so that in bad weather we could play ballgames inside – we played football, dodge-ball and even French cricket in there. As you left the playroom and turned left there was an office. Next to the office, at the foot of the stairs, was the sewing room. To the right of the stairs was a corridor which led to the back door, and to the right of this corridor, opposite the playroom, was the dining room.

When you entered the back corridor there were cupboards on both sides which belonged to the domestic staff. Off this corridor you found the downstairs toilet and boot-room, there were lots of pigeon-holes in this room where we would keep our outdoor shoes, and there was also a row of cupboards for our school Burberrys and wellie-boots. Below this room was the boiler room. As you left this part of the corridor you would come to the back door. To the left of the door was a very cold room where all the perishable food was kept until the cook, Mrs Hall, needed it. To the right of the back door was another small hallway which brought you to the back stairs.

Underneath these stairs was a walk-in cupboard where the hoovers and cleaning equipment were kept. At the foot of the back stairs there was a large cupboard which never seemed to have anything in it but there was a large bell placed on top of it which was used to call us in for mealtimes and to bring us all together at other times when necessary. There was also another large glass door to the dining room at the foot of these stairs.

To reach the kitchen you had to go along yet another corridor. On the right was the staff sitting-room and dining room and opposite these were two more rooms. One was used for washing the dishes (we had a kind of sterilizer for the crockery and cutlery), and the other room was where the crockery was kept. The kitchen lay at the end of the corridor and off the kitchen there were two pantries. One was used for preparing the food and vegetables and the other for washing the kitchen utensils. The kitchen had its own back door with its own vestibule where the milk was delivered each morning. Outside the back door was a veranda which hung over the two rooms, pantries and larder.

Outside, beyond the kitchen back door, was a row of outbuildings which the gardener used as his potting sheds and to keep his equipment in. The outbuildings were in a courtyard with a garage which had very tall arched doors where Miss Martin kept her car. There were stables here too.

Attached to the garage were the laundry rooms. One room was used for washing with a row of Belfast sinks along the side wall. These sinks had their own built-in scrubbing boards. At the other side of the room there was a very large industrial washing machine and a huge spin dryer and at one end of the room rows of pulleys hung from the ceiling. The other room was used as the ironing room with two large ironing tables and more pulleys to hold all the ironed sheets, pillowcases and numerous clothes.

Outside the laundry rooms were the drying green, back drive and playing fields. The children mainly used the back drive for going to school and church, we were also taught to cycle in the back drive, and I remember that there was a fence which bordered the entire back drive and all round our playing field.

The field had a large sandpit just over the hedge from the laundry rooms and at the top left of the field were our swings and roundabout. We also had a pavilion in the playing field, and to the left of the swings was our orchard with our woods to the very back of the field. Coming back to the field and over the fence was our gardener's cottage, and as you walked back towards Tenterfield, in another part of the field was a hen run.

Opposite this was the beginning of the front garden and in this part stood a very large and old greenhouse. Straight ahead you came to the sunken garden which brought you to the front of the house, and behind the potting sheds was the vegetable garden.

Second Floor

At the top of the front stairs was Miss Martin's bedroom and sitting room, and to the right of these were three long, wide steps which led to the boys' bedroom. These rooms looked onto the front and side gardens. The side bedroom was above the playroom and there was another boys' bedroom above the front door. In the front hall, to the left of the long steps were another three steps. These led towards the girls' area. This part of the house looked more like servants quarters but was still very nice. Then there was yet another corridor where Miss Martin's bathroom was with a boys' toilet at the other end.

When you came to the end of this corridor there was a large landing which brought you back to the back stairs. Standing on this landing was a very large wardrobe where spare clothes were kept and to the right of this wardrobe was the door into the toilets and baths. If I remember correctly there were only five baths but one in particular was very large.

Passing the wardrobe and going towards the girls' room you came to a two-roomed bedroom for the older girls and further along the corridor you came to what we all called the baby room. You then went along another small corridor and came to the girls' dormitory which was entered by a door which had steps down into this very large room. This room was above the kitchen. Going back along the corridors to the landing which housed the wardrobe you came to the back stairs which went up one more flight or down to the ground floor. Halfway down these stairs leading to the ground floor there were other stairs leading off on the right-hand side, I think there were about six stairs and they took you up to a bathroom and two sickrooms. The first room could take four beds but up another few stairs was another sickroom which also had a door into Miss Martin's sitting-room.

Going back to the landing for the back stairs, you climbed up more stairs until halfway up you came to yet another set of stairs on the left which led to a bathroom and a large bedroom that the frauleins used. By this stage you were almost at the top of the house. The top floor had another bedroom to the left of the stairs and another corridor with built-in cupboards took you to the older girls' bedroom which could sleep about four. This was my favourite room. It had 'the round window' (which is still there today) to the side of the room and a large window to the back of the house. When there were more older boys than girls, the boys would have this room. Going back along the corridor you would come to Mackie's bathroom and the girls' bathroom. There was one further small, narrow flight of stairs left, these were very creaky with the walls and treads all made from wood, leading to another room. Mackie called it her square turret and, as can be seen on the photo of the house, this was at the front of the house.

Appendix 2: Tenterfield History

John Christie (1824-1902) was born in Perthshire and spent his working life as a coal master at Arniston Colliery Midlothian. In 1892 he opened an orphanage in Portobello, Inverey Home.

He bought Tenterfield House, Dunbar Road, Haddington in 1897 and opened it as a home for girls in 1898. Christie died in 1902 but he left money to maintain the Christie homes in his will. In addition to Tenterfield 2 other homes were opened in Haddington: Templedean, which was adjacent to Tenterfield opened in 1903, and Carmendean , which opened in 1912.

Carmendean was built in the grounds of Tenterfield – it was necessary to build this home because Inverey Home at Portobello had closed. At the same time a school was also built in the grounds. In 1920 the Trustees purchased 2 Tantallon Terrace, North Berwick as a holiday home for the girls.

In 1928 an Act of Parliament amalgamated the Christie Homes into the Lothian Homes Trust. Carmendean and Templedean homes closed in the 1950s Templedean was later converted into flats (Templedean Hall) and Carmendean became a Nursing Home (Templedean Nursing Home). Tenterfield remained a children's home until c1992 but from c1950 was run by the local authority rather than the Lothian Homes Trust. The local authority responsible was the Midlothian, East Lothian & Peebles County Council Social Work Committee, and from Local Government reorganisation in 1975 the Lothian Regional Council Social Work Committee.

Lothian Homes Trust still exists as a charity. It provides a range of services to young people aged 16-22 in the Edinburgh and surrounding area at risk of homelessness and social exclusion.

Records

Register "The Christie Female Industrial Home – Register of Inmates" (covers all 3 homes)	C1929-1960s	Callum Kennedy, Partner Lindsays Solicitors, Edinburgh (per records of the Lothian Homes Trust) 0131 229 1212
Auld Aquaintance Magazine (Magazine of the Old Girls Association)	1931-1935	Local History Centre, Haddington
Tenterfield Visitors Book		Found in Lothian Villa, now with Ross

		Ireland
House Meetings Book (Tenterfield)		Found in Lothian Villa, now with Ross Ireland
Tenterfield House Education Department Inspector's Reports ((ED11/543)	1955-1968	National Archives of Scotland

Sources

Gray, Alastair H, "Roots Going Deep East Lothian Church History", June 1996

Baker, Sonia (Editor), East Lothian 1945-2000 Fourth Statistical Account Volume Two

Files on 'Christie Homes' and 'Tenterfield House', Local History Service (these include extracts from the Haddington Courier).